To: Sher Bean

From: Duberdov
Christmas 2018

Words
to Calm
Your Heart

DEVOTIONAL

Ellie Claire
gift & paper expressions

Ellie Claire® Gift & Paper Expressions
Franklin, TN 37067
EllieClaire.com
Ellie Claire is a registered trademark of Worthy Media, Inc.

Words to Calm Your Heart Devotional Journal
© 2017 by Ellie Claire
Published by Ellie Claire, an imprint of Worthy Publishing Group, a division of Worthy
Media, Inc.

ISBN 978-1-63326-161-7

Stock or custom editions of Ellie Claire titles may be purchased in bulk for educational,
business, ministry, fundraising, or sales promotional use. For information, please e-mail
info@EllieClaire.com

Illustrations: Kenna Sato Designs and Margarita Manish of creativemarket.com;
shutterstock.com

Compiled by Jill Jones
Cover and interior design by Melissa Reagan

Printed in China

1 2 3 4 5 6 7 8 9 – 21 20 19 18 17

Contents

Fear not, for I am with you;
be not dismayed, for I am your God.
I will strengthen you, yes,
I will help you,
I will uphold you with
My righteous right hand.

ISAIAH 41:10 NKJV

Seeing Clearly

*Then will the eyes of the blind be opened
and the ears of the deaf unstopped.*

ISAIAH 35:5 NIV

Weeks before leaving on a mission trip, I couldn't find a document I needed to receive a new passport. I searched in every drawer, folder, and pile of papers in the house. Nothing.

Exhausted, I stopped and prayed, calming myself down. I went back to the first place I looked, my "important papers" drawer, and the document was right there.

Problems can strike like lightning, blinding us to the truth right before our eyes. If a friend doesn't return your call, they may be having a bad week. If you're passed up for a promotion, a better position may be waiting. Like my missing document that wasn't really missing, you may not know the whole story.

When trouble rushes in, take a breath and ask God to uncover your eyes. Let yourself be like the blind man healed by Jesus in Bethsaida: "Once more Jesus put his hands on the man's eyes. Then his eyes were opened, his sight was restored, and he saw everything clearly" (Mark 8:25 NIV).

Father, give me Your heavenly vision
so I can see beyond the surface
of situations, never losing hope.

I keep asking that the God of our Lord Jesus Christ, the
glorious Father, may give you the Spirit of wisdom and
revelation, so that you may know him better. I pray that the
eyes of your heart may be enlightened in order that you may
know the hope to which he has called you, the riches of his
glorious inheritance in his holy people

EPHESIANS 1:17–18 NIV

Heaven often seems distant and unknown,
but if He who made the road...is our guide,
we need not fear to lose the way.

HENRY VAN DYKE

Dinner Prayer

The Lord gives strength to his people;
the Lord blesses his people with peace.

PSALM 29:11 NIV

My prayer was simple: "Lord, please let dinner be peaceful." My two sons had reached the age when they considered bickering a sport, and the dinner table was prime battleground. They were quick to argue with each other over any little thing and to complain about the food. At the time, my wife was suffering with a painful hip condition, so I was the cook. As I prepared the meal, I prayed for God to give us a dinner experience akin to the *Brady Bunch*, although I knew my entrée wouldn't go over as well as Alice's always did.

Once everything was ready, I put the meal on the table and called everyone to supper. The boys bounded in and sat down, and I said grace. Much to my surprise, my sons engaged in pleasant conversation. My wife and I asked about their day, and they shared positive things about school and funny stories about their classmates. I even received compliments about the food. In my heart, I gave thanks to God.

It was a lovely, peaceful evening and proof that God provides peace when we ask. Even if it's for something as small as relief from sibling rivalry, He hears and cares about every aspect of our lives.

Lord, remind me to pray for peace as needed
and to thank You when it comes.

All that is good, all that is true, all that is beautiful,
all that is beneficent, be it great or small,
be it perfect or fragmentary, natural as well as supernatural,
moral as well as material, comes from God.

JOHN HENRY NEWMAN

Ask, and it will be given to you;
seek, and you will find; knock, and it will
be opened to you. For everyone who asks
receives, and the one who seeks finds,
and to the one who knocks it will be opened.

MATTHEW 7:7–8 ESV

A Cardinal in the Night

Give thanks to the God of heaven,
for his steadfast love endures forever.

PSALM 136:17 NIV

The fear I had battled since leaving the hospital won a momentary victory. I had been alone before, but tonight was different. Tonight thoughts of losing God's greatest earthly gift and being left alone as a widow terrified and filled me with anxiety.

Outside our dark and empty home, I opened the car door, closed it again, and sat there until the car lights dimmed and went out. I cried, prayed, and cried some more. When I reached in the glove compartment for a tissue, I noticed something oddly aglow in the distance.

I walked through the garden and sighed with delight at the solar lantern my husband had assembled and hung there. Glowing in the dark of night was a stained glass cardinal—a bird that holds special meaning to me as a reminder of God's presence, protection, and steadfast love.

When we cry out to God, anxious over situations beyond our control, He hears and floods our hearts and minds with the gift of His supernatural peace. That peace can come in many forms, including a garden lantern and cardinal glowing in the night.

O Lord, when anxious thoughts
surround and bind me, remind me
of Your promised peace through Jesus.

God is our refuge and strength, an ever-present
help in trouble. Therefore we will not fear.

PSALM 46:1–2 NIV

If God be our God, He will give us peace
in trouble. When there is a storm without,
He will make peace within.
The world can create trouble in peace,
but God can create peace in trouble.

THOMAS WATSON

A Reflection of Hope

May the God of hope fill you with all joy and peace
as you trust in him, so that you may overflow
with hope by the power of the Holy Spirit.

ROMANS 15:13 NIV

I'm not a poet, but I went to Ethel's poetry workshop to hear her soothing voice. Back at home my world was unraveling, to the point where being at a five-day writers' conference felt like a vacation.

Fifteen years earlier Ethel and I had prayed together for the first time and she had given me a verse—Romans 15:13. Since then she'd been a faithful source of gentle, Godly wisdom, encouragement, and prayer. Now I was fighting a personal battle and she was battling cancer. Sitting in her workshop, I felt the hope and peace of Romans 15:13 that Ethel reflected. I thanked God for her friendship and the deeper faith she inspired at a time when I desperately needed hope and peace. Between her and other sisters in Christ, I left the conference strengthened for the next step.

In life's difficult moments we need friends who not only tell us the truth but make God's truth real to us. How precious it is when we find one whose presence alone comforts our spirit.

Lord, help me to seek out friends
who reflect Your peace.

Above all things have fervent love for one another, for "love will cover a multitude of sins." Be hospitable to one another without grumbling. As each one has received a gift, minister it to one another, as good stewards of the manifold grace of God.

1 PETER 4:8–10 NKJV

At times our own light goes out
and is rekindled by a spark from another
person. Each of us has cause to think
with deep gratitude of those who have
lighted the flame within us.

ALBERT SCHWEITZER

God Fights for Us!

Do not be in dread or afraid of them. The Lord your God who goes before you will himself fight for you.

DEUTERONOMY 1:29–30 ESV

Have you ever heard the expression "Don't bring a knife to a gunfight"? It's an interesting idiom and works well in this passage. The truth is that we need to be adequately prepared for spiritual battles in our lives, and we are insufficient in our own strength to fight. The Lord our God will fight for us and we are not to be afraid of the war that rages.

As we face an enemy who is greater than us, we grapple with just how weak we are. But our peace comes from knowing that no matter what battle we may face—physical, emotional, mental, or spiritual—the ultimate warrior, our God, goes before us and fights for us. We can take the next step in our daily lives and not fear what lies in front of us. As a matter of fact, we can live in joy while we walk the path God has set for us. Free from the fears that so easily weigh us down, we grasp hold of the purpose that we are here to fulfill, leaving the battle in God's hands.

Thank You, Lord, for going before us and
fighting the battles only You can win!

Not by might, nor by power, but by my Spirit,
says the Lord of hosts.

ZECHARIAH 4:6 ESV

If you are at a place in your life where you feel
like you can't take one step without the Lord's help,
be glad. He has you where He wants you.

STORMIE OMARTIAN

The Lord will fight for you;
you need only to be still.

EXODUS 14:14 NIV

God Is My Protector

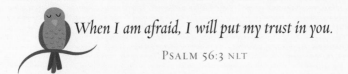 *When I am afraid, I will put my trust in you.*

PSALM 56:3 NLT

Fear is a primal emotion. When we give in to it, we lose all perspective. When we turn away from it, life once again regains the balance God promises. I found that out one cold winter day. I received an email accusing me of horrible things—things I hadn't done but couldn't prove. With that one email, every fear I'd ever had became real. I sobbed, and I prayed, but I couldn't tear myself away from the fear.

I began to fixate on the accusations, rehearsing all the things that could come. I devised possible scenarios and tried to find a way out of that tunnel of terror. I only found my way from that terrible place with the help of two pieces of advice. My friend urged me to begin playing uplifting music and writing out Bible verses that promised God's protection. By doing this, I moved my focus to God instead of the fear.

This lesson has stood the test of time. I learned that choosing to trust God changes our perspective and gives us the strength to persevere.

Dear Lord, don't let me give in to my fears.
Instead, stand in front of me, and let me see
the peace I crave. Amen.

Have I not commanded you? Be strong and courageous.
Do not be frightened, and do not be dismayed,
for the Lord your God is with you wherever you go.

JOSHUA 1:9 ESV

If I could hear Christ praying for me
in the next room, I would not fear
a million enemies. Yet distance makes
no difference. He is praying for me.

ROBERT MURRAY McCHEYNE

Whisper Words of Wisdom

The Lord says, "Forget what happened before,
and do not think about the past. Look at the new thing
I am going to do. It is already happening. Don't you see it?

ISAIAH 43:18–19 NCV

I was out in the world alone for the first time and caught up in a lifestyle that left me feeling completely out of control. I got a tattoo. It was the ever-famous Beatles lyric "Let it be," a perfect reminder to let go and stop trying to control everything.

And now I can never win an argument again in my life. When my blood pressure rises, when my fur bristles, when I grasp at dominance, a sly smile creeps across my husband's face, and he whispers, "Let it be."

Sometimes I want to hoard my frustration. To keep it for myself and leverage it to micromanage those around me. But I can't control a situation—or a person—when I actually let go. Letting it be is always the freer thing. God's whisper of wisdom is doing a new thing in me. Only when we let go of the twisted tendency to control people and things can we have the freedom of abundant life.

God of peace, in my hour of darkness,
You are standing right in front of me,
doing a new thing. Help me to let it be
so that I may be free in Your love.

Abide in Me, and I in you. As the branch cannot
bear fruit of itself, unless it abides in the vine,
neither can you, unless you abide in Me.

JOHN 15:4 NKJV

Real contentment must come from within.
You and I cannot change or control the
world around us, but we can change and
control the world within us.

WARREN WIERSBE

It's Quiet in Here

He prepared the inner sanctuary within the temple
to set the ark of the covenant of the LORD.

1 KINGS 6:19 NIV

It's a noisy world we live in—uneasy, impatient, and dissatisfied. Maybe it's always been that way, but to this extreme? Everyone's in a hurry, and no one seems to remember the subtle consideration of yesterday. Remember when we used to dole out grace by the cup full, offer a helping hand to a stranger, or make time to wait within our busy schedules? What's happened to us? Have we become numb to our animated surroundings, or perhaps deaf to the piercing sound of people's frustration?

Sweet is the silent stream that meanders through God's property—that inner place where we can enter, day or night, to take cover in His still serenity. A refuge where the walls are high and indestructible. A retreat where no person, problem, or pain will find you. A spiritual Fort Knox of impenetrable peace that lives within you, if only you will step inside and close the door—tightly. Friend, relax, leave the turmoil outside, and safely shelter in God's quiet place.

God, help me to find that inner peace amid the noise of today. Help me to rest with calm assurance that I am safe inside Your sanctuary. Amen.

If you refuse to be hurried and pressed, if you stay your soul on God, nothing can keep you from that clearness of spirit which is life and peace. In that stillness you know what His will is.

AMY CARMICHAEL

God never asked us to meet life's pressures and demands on our own terms or by relying upon our own strength. Nor did He demand that we win His favor by assembling an impressive portfolio of good deeds. Instead, He invites us to enter His rest.

CHARLES R. SWINDOLL

Take a Deep Breath

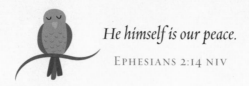

He himself is our peace.

EPHESIANS 2:14 NIV

She sat across the coffee table, pouring out a story of conflict, deceit, and frustration. The international adoption of her daughter had been delayed, and nearly derailed, by a midlevel bureaucrat who seemed to be exceeding her authority by a considerable degree.

Now my parishioner asked for advice. Should she press her concerns to a higher level, perhaps even bring a lawsuit, as some had suggested? Did she owe it to other families to expose this injustice? She was deeply conflicted.

I offered a simple question. "Is this something God wants you to do, or is it something others are asking of you?"

Her shoulders relaxed, and the tension drained from her face. Her answer had become clear.

Stress comes from taking on burdens that Jesus never asked us to carry. We labor to demonstrate our value to employers, neighbors, and even ourselves, convinced we have something to prove. But Jesus never asks us to validate ourselves. His acceptance is unconditional, and His reward is rest. So rest.

*Lord, free me from my need to prove
my worth, and enable me to rest
in the peace You have given.*

Come to me, all of you who are weary and carry heavy
burdens, and I will give you rest. Take my yoke upon you.
Let me teach you, because I am humble and gentle at heart,
and you will find rest for your souls. For my yoke
is easy to bear, and the burden I give you is light.

MATTHEW 11:28–30 NLT

*Most of the things we need to be
most fully alive never come in busyness.
They grow in rest.*

MARK BUCHANAN

Touchstones of Peace

*The LORD said to him, "Peace be to you. Do not fear;
you shall not die." Then Gideon built an altar there
to the LORD and called it, The LORD Is Peace.*

JUDGES 6:23–24 ESV

Gideon's world is in shambles. His way of life is being threatened by the presence of the Midianites who are attempting to take over Israel. What's more, Scripture tells us he is part of the weakest tribe and the least in his father's household. As if he weren't stressed out enough already, the angel of the Lord appears and tells him that he will be the one to deliver Israel from the hand of the Midianites.

Gideon asks the Lord for a sign. After the Lord performs it, Gideon is flooded with peace and he does something interesting: he builds an altar and calls it The Lord is Peace. It's a memorial to his anxiety, a physical reminder of the peace and comfort the Lord has given him.

Can you think of a time when your world was in chaos? How can you create a touchstone of peace today to remind you of God's presence in the midst of anxiety?

*Prince of Peace, You are sovereign over all.
Bring peace into my chaos. Remind me
of Your past provisions of peace, and give
me hope in my current circumstances.*

My Lord God, I have no idea where I am going.
I do not see the road ahead of me. I cannot know
for certain where it will end…. But I believe that
the desire to please You does in fact please You.
And I hope I have that desire in all that I am doing.
I hope that I will never do anything apart from that desire.
And I know that if I do this, You will lead me by the right
road though I may know nothing about it. Therefore will
I trust You always, though I may seem to be lost and in the
shadow of death. I will not fear, for You are ever with me.
And You will never leave me to face my perils alone.

THOMAS MERTON

The Answer to My Fear

*I sought the Lord, and He answered me
and delivered me from all my fears.*

PSALM 34:4 HCSB

I'm a person who craves order. No matter the circumstance, I want to know what's coming so I can have a plan in place. Yep, you guessed it, I'm a card-carrying control freak. This is never more evident than when I'm afraid. In the past, my way of coping with fear was to look for answers—remedies—to alleviate my fears. I'd worry over every detail of what might happen, mapping out scenarios and ways to cope. It was exhausting to me—and to those around me.

One morning, I read this verse and it seemed to leap off the page at me. Could it be this simple? Hesitantly, I began to pray. I asked God to take my fear and replace it with His peace. He immediately answered me, enveloping me in His presence and His peace. The circumstances hadn't changed, but I had.

In turning to Him, I acknowledged that even if I don't have all the answers, God does. And He's big enough, wise enough, and loving enough to carry me through any scenario.

Dear Lord, help me to always turn
to You first when I'm afraid
and looking for answers. Amen.

If God be our God, He will give us peace in trouble.
When there is a storm without, He will make peace within.
The world can create trouble in peace,
but God can create peace in trouble.

THOMAS WATSON

God has not given us a spirit of fear,
but of power and of love
and of a sound mind.

2 TIMOTHY 1:7 NKJV

Retraining Your Mind

Cast all your anxiety on him because he cares for you.

1 PETER 5:7 NIV

Like muddy paw prints on a newly waxed floor, the cares of life can prance into our well-ordered world. Hopeful morning breaths clog inside of us. Worries build to pressure cooker temperature as we fret.

Fussing over problems feels natural. Required. But anxious thoughts don't solve anything. In them we find no helpful perspective. No comforting reassurance. Anxiety only confirms we are stressed—which we already knew!

The psalmist poured his complaints before the same God who welcomes us to give Him our struggles. But like the poet-king, we don't stop with the grumbling. Instead we pause and trust our good God. He's proven faithful time and again, handling the messy parts of life. We step into peace as He invites us to release problems and anxiety into His capable care. He loves us and is pleased to help.

Sometimes He solves everything in a snap; usually He invites us to grab hold of His strong hand, walk a little slower, and just breathe. He sees the bigger perspective and works for good. As His plan unfolds He is with us. His loving care comforts. His wisdom guides. His confidence reassures. His strength uplifts.

Dear Jesus, thank You for taking
my anxiety and replacing it with peace.

A Christian's freedom from anxiety is not due to some
guaranteed freedom from trouble, but to the folly of worry
and especially to the confidence that God is our Father, that
even permitted suffering is within the orbit of His care.

JOHN STOTT

I am still confident of this:
I will see the goodness
of the Lord in the land of the living.
Wait for the Lord; be strong and take heart
and wait for the Lord.

PSALM 27:13–14 NIV

Pause for a Time-In

I have calmed and quieted myself...
like a weaned child I am content.

PSALM 131:2 NIV

Ever been sent to time-out? As the beloved of Christ, we can enjoy time-*in*. Time-outs put us on the couch, in the corner, or at the back of the classroom, but time-ins can happen *anywhere*. In the shower. On the freeway. When we wait for a doctor's appointment. Even in a room full of people.

Time-ins can last thirty seconds or two hours. We can enjoy a time-in many times every day.

A time-in is simply a pause to embrace complete dependence on Jesus and all He does for us. It's a moment to remember you're *all in* with Him, and He's *all in* with you. We let go of faults because they're already forgiven. We cease striving. After all, He planted the Holy Spirit within us, and He's empowering us to do good. When we take a time-in, we remember that.

Time-ins refocus swirling thoughts to trust. Time-ins replace guilt and striving with peace. Time-ins receive and offer love. Time-ins invite quiet strength as we reflect on God and our complete dependence on Him.

Here I am, Jesus, taking a time-in and remembering all You've done for me.

Rest time is not waste time. It is economy to gather fresh strength.... It is wisdom to take occasional furlough. In the long run, we shall do more by sometimes doing less.

CHARLES SPURGEON

Yes, my soul, find rest in God; my hope comes from him. Truly he is my rock and my salvation; he is my fortress, I will not be shaken.

PSALM 62:5–6 NIV

Should we feel at times disheartened and
discouraged, a simple movement of heart
toward God will renew our powers.
Whatever He may demand of us,
He will give us at the moment
the strength and courage that we need.

FRANÇOIS FÉNELON

Let Jesus Move Your Mountain

> *"Not by might nor by power, but by my Spirit,"*
> *says the Lord Almighty.*
>
> ZECHARIAH 4:6 NIV

Close your eyes and look at your mountain—that very large thing that's keeping you from moving forward. Is it fear or anger? Maybe a health issue or personal dilemma. Whatever it is, it's big! And after doing everything in your power to change it, sweet talk it, beat it senseless, or ignore it, you end up exhausted and suddenly aware that it's simply too mammoth for you to lift.

Friend, don't you know that anything God has put your name on never requires force? He is the Lord of the meek; the Prince of Peace; the One who said, *"Be still, and know I am God!"* In our fiercest efforts to move things around, we take the responsibility away from the One who allowed them there in the first place. What God requires from us is to hand over everything to Him...*everything*. It's grace that we don't have to fight for what belongs to us. Jesus will handle it, so just sit back and let your Son of Man do the heavy lifting!

My dear God, in all of my crazy effort,
I somehow forgot that You are in control.
Remind me that I don't have to be strong
when it's Jesus moving the mountains. Amen.

He said to me, "My grace is sufficient for you,
for My strength is made perfect in weakness."
Therefore most gladly I will rather boast in my infirmities,
that the power of Christ may rest upon me.

2 CORINTHIANS 12:9 NKJV

Don't tell God how big your mountain is.
Tell your mountain how big your God is.

Trust God to Work It Out

Peacemakers who sow in peace reap a harvest of righteousness.

JAMES 3:18 NIV

Nothing good happens at two o'clock in the morning, especially when you're lying awake, too stressed to sleep because of a relational conflict. I'd been anxious over an issue for weeks, feeling helpless, angry, and overloaded.

"Just let it go," friends told me. It was good advice, but I didn't know how. As I lay watching the clock turn another hour, God finally got my attention.

"Do you believe I have your best at heart?"

"Yes, Lord, of course."

"And do you believe that I want justice, even more than you do?"

"Yes."

"Then why won't you trust Me on this one?"

I had no answer. When I make it my responsibility to ensure that others behave well, I feel anxiety. There's no way I can balance the scales for the whole universe. I only exhaust myself in the process.

Yet when I seek peace, I find peace—not just in relationships but in my spirit as well.

God promises a blessing for those who seek peace. Those driven by revenge or retaliation find only heartache. Trade in your bitterness for a good night's sleep.

Lord, help me to let go of my need to be right and hold on to Your righteousness.

Seek peace and pursue it.

Psalm 34:14 niv

Where the soul is full of peace and joy, outward surroundings and circumstances are of comparatively little account.

Hannah Whitall Smith

Look at those who are honest and good, for a wonderful future awaits those who love peace.

Psalm 37:37 nlt

The Peaceful Presence of His Guiding Spirit

Then he breathed on them and said, "Receive the Holy Spirit."

JOHN 20:22 NLT

Ah! Do you feel it? It's the peaceful presence of God living right there inside you. When you received Jesus, this Comforter moved in. He's called the Holy Spirit, and He lives in the center of your being. Always. Nothing makes Him leave. He's excited about developing God's personality within you. One of the ways He makes you more like Himself is by making you more peaceful.

He likes it when you're at peace. He likes to see you restful and confident. Then you're living like He does.

He's given you a lot to be confident about. Like the fact that He's promised to guide you by His peaceful presence. Take a calming breath. Do you sense the peace? Release any anxious thought into His care. Trust that He's going to show you how to handle any struggle, how to walk through any chaos. When you're not sure how to respond to something, being still and evaluating which choices bring you peace are good ways to discern how the Holy Spirit is leading you.

He's not worried. He knows He's got this.

You know that too.

Thank You, Holy Spirit, for moving in
and giving me confidence that You'll lead me
as I rest in Your peaceful presence.

I am no longer anxious about anything, as I realize
the Lord is able to carry out His will, and His will is mine.
It makes no matter where He places me, or how.
That is rather for Him to consider than for me;
for in the easiest positions He must give me His grace,
and in the most difficult, His grace is sufficient.

HUDSON TAYLOR

May the God of hope fill you with
all joy and peace as you trust in him,
so that you may overflow with hope
by the power of the Holy Spirit.

ROMANS 15:13 NIV

Escape to Jesus

For you are my safe refuge,
a fortress where my enemies cannot reach me.

PSALM 61:3 NLT

Ever feel like you need a long, luxurious vacation? Like you need to rest in a cabin for a week or two, far from the demands of daily life?

Feelings of being overwhelmed can attack us, and life has a way of leaving us strung out, hankering for a beach vacation. When constant overload and stress strike, resist the temptation to tune out. Instead, tune in to Jesus.

We find the same relaxation at the feet of Jesus and can escape to Him every day. We don't need a cabin in the woods or a house on the beach to find the kind of soul rest we need. We don't even need a three-day weekend to find peace. Jesus offers a way to unwind in His presence.

We can pour out our cares to the One who cares for us. Amid daily pressures, Jesus offers refuge. We can cling to Him during stressful seasons.

Jesus offers abundant life on this earth. Let His life bubble up in you today, washing away anxiety and stress. Say good-bye to overwhelm and hello to the rest only God can bring.

Jesus, teach us to escape to You,
not to things of the world.

I have come that they may have life,
and that they may have it more abundantly.

JOHN 10:10 NKJV

If you look at the world, you'll be distressed.
If you look within, you'll be depressed.
But if you look at Christ, you'll be at rest.

CORRIE TEN BOOM

You have made us for Yourself, O Lord,
and our heart is restless until it rests in You.

ST. AUGUSTINE

Pouring Out a Waterfall

Trust in him at all times, O people; pour out your heart before him; God is a refuge for us. Selah.

PSALM 62:8 ESV

We took our kids on a cross country road trip this past spring, trekking from the West Coast to the East Coast, and back again. One of our last stops was spent exploring Yellowstone National Park. Besides the otherworldly geothermal pools, a favorite stop was the vista above the Upper Falls of the Yellowstone River. The enormous waterfall cascades 109 feet, crashing into the gorge of Yellowstone's Grand Canyon.

This is the picture that comes to mind when I consider pouring out my heart to the Lord. When I am desperately seeking refuge, when life is full of churning whitewater, I need to know I have a Father who can handle the raging deluge.

Not only is He able to receive all we pour out, He transforms our splashing chaos into beauty.

Sometimes He does this by slowing the rush to a calm stream, like the glassy tributaries that meander across Yellowstone's grassy meadows. Other times He strengthens our banks, enabling us to sustain the surge, giving others a chance to bask breathless in the beauty and wonder of a person surrendered to His will.

Father, I pour out the rushing waters
of my heart to You. Give peace,
strength, and redeeming beauty.

Because of the empty tomb, we have peace.
Because of His resurrection, we can have peace during
even the most troubling of times because we know
He is in control of all that happens in the world.

PAUL CHAPPELL

Open your mouth and taste, open your eyes
and see how good God is. Blessed are you
who run to him. Worship God
if you want the best; worship opens
doors to all his goodness.

PSALM 34:8–9 MSG

Have I Been Here Before?

He brought me forth also into a large place;
he delivered me, because he delighted in me.

PSALM 18:19 KJV

Sometimes the only way to move forward is to look back.

The cares of work and family and money and health seem too heavy. Tension tightens the cords in your neck and presses against your temples and you wonder how you can shoulder any more.

Stop and ask: *Have I been here before? Have I experienced this in the past?* Yes. I've carried these burdens before. I've felt this anxiety. *What happened the last time?* I called out to God and He heard my cry. He gave me His peace. He brought me through it. He will again. Because He delights in me.

It takes discipline and practice to stop and look back, to remember God's faithfulness, to focus on the fact that He delights in you. Take a few minutes every day this week to write out some verses that bring to mind God's peace and presence—verses like Matthew 11:28: "Come to me, all who labor and are heavy laden, and I will give you rest." Carry them with you for those times when you need to be reminded.

*Lord, in those times when our cares
seem too heavy, help us to turn to You
and recall Your faithfulness.*

The Lord your God is living among you.
He is a mighty savior. He will take delight in you
with gladness. With his love, he will calm all your fears.
He will rejoice over you with joyful songs.

ZEPHANIAH 3:17 NLT

May grace and peace be multiplied to you
in the knowledge of God and of Jesus our Lord.

2 PETER 1:2 ESV

*No circumstance is so big
that He cannot control it.*

JERRY BRIDGES

Resting in Our Refuge

The LORD is good, a refuge in times of trouble.
He cares for those who trust in him.

NAHUM 1:7 NIV

He loves you, you know. He sees you. When you laugh and your heart is full. And in those awful times when it hurts so much you go numb.

He enjoys the happy days with you. He loves it when you dance in joy, and sends the sweetness of His presence to increase your mutual delight. He also understands your fight to trust Him on the bad days, and He comes whispering love and peace. *"Remember My goodness,"* He says. *"I'm dedicated to meeting you right there in the middle of the trouble."*

He's not far away. In fact, He's as close as your very breath.

Do you sense His whisper? *"Make Me your refuge,"* He says. *"I am your strong tower. I am the rock where you stand steady. I shelter you beneath My wings. Even as a nursing momma never forgets her baby, I can never forget you. I stand like a momma bear over you. I am here. Always."*

Take a deep breath. Let His love penetrate the chaos. Let Him still the storm within your heart.

He is good. He will never abandon you. He cares about everything you care about.

You are my refuge, Lord, and I trust You.

Can a mother forget her nursing child?
Can she feel no love for the child she has borne?
But even if that were possible, I would not forget you!
See, I have written your name on the palms of my hands.

ISAIAH 49:15–16 NLT

We should be astonished at the goodness of
God, stunned that He should bother to call
us by name, our mouths wide open at His
love, bewildered that at this very moment
we are standing on holy ground.

BRENNAN MANNING

For the Overwhelmed, Worried, and Discouraged

*You, O Lord, are a shield around me; you are my glory,
the one who holds my head high.*

PSALM 3:3 NLT

When we feel overwhelmed, when it seems life is on the offensive and we're assailed by the fiery darts of the enemy: the Lord is our shield. He surrounds us with His presence. There are no chinks in this protection. He will not allow anything to harm us not meant for our ultimate good. We need not fear any attack.

When we feel worried over what others think, when we feel our reputation is under scrutiny or our good name is wrongly maligned: the Lord is our glory. We don't need to strive to make everyone happy. We have nothing to prove. His glory is complete and sufficient; we need only to trust and obey.

When we feel discouraged, downtrodden, as if we're carrying the weight of our world on our shoulders: the Lord is the lifter of our head. He reaches out to us, gently invites us to lift our eyes up from our difficult circumstances and look full in His wonderful face. We need not let our circumstances have the final say, but instead meet His loving gaze and be filled with peace.

Tender Father, make us sensitive to Your
presence. Fill us with confidence in Your
protection, and replace our anxiety
with Your perfect peace.

The Lord is my strength and my shield;
in him my heart trusts, and I am helped;
my heart exults, and with my song I give thanks to him.

PSALM 28:7 ESV

When we appropriate God's great
enablers His grace and His peace
we can achieve gentleness and calmness
even during hard times.

KAY ARTHUR

Peace in Chaos

Now may the Lord of peace himself give you peace at all times and in every way. The Lord be with all of you.

2 THESSALONIANS 3:16 NIV

Chaos seems to follow me like a lost puppy. It shows up as a sick child at the wrong time, or a lost job in the midst of new beginnings, or a lost parent during a child's rebellion and a move all at the same time. I must be a chaos magnet and as I grow older the magnet seems to get stronger. But chaos, unlike a cute puppy, is not a welcome visitor in my life.

The chaos may manifest in different ways but my peace always remains the same. God is a constant companion of mine and He is consistent. In a moment's time, my day can go sideways and God can set me back upright with one Scripture from His amazing Word.

Because I trust in Him, I can always know that in everything, at all times, in every way His peace is assured and in His peace I am secure.

Father God, Your peace is all I need. I trust in You to provide the peace that surpasses all understanding at all times in my life. When chaos comes, cover me in Your peace. In Jesus's name, amen.

It is God who arms me with strength and keeps my way secure. He makes my feet like the feet of a deer; he causes me to stand on the heights.

PSALM 18:32–33 NIV

God has not promised sun without rain, joy without sorrow, peace without pain. But God has promised strength for the day, rest for the labor, light for the way, grace for the trials, help from above, unfailing sympathy, undying love.

ANNIE JOHNSON FLINT

Perfect Peace

*Thou wilt keep him in perfect peace
whose mind is stayed on thee.*

ISAIAH 26:3 KJV

The worst is when you can't sleep. The turmoil and troubles you've dealt with during the day rob you of rest at night. They fight it out while you try to shut them out; they replay themselves with the "if only" and "how dare they" commentaries attached.

But God's Word offers a better rest, a sweeter peace. He promises that we can quiet our restless spirits with His spirit of rest. He offers "peace that passes understanding" and "peace, not as the world gives." His peace is perfect.

So what do we do to find that perfect peace? Keep our minds on Him. We must focus on God's power, not the tumultuous circumstances. We fix our hearts on Him so that He can fix what concerns us. We stay our thoughts on our faithful Father, who does all things well. This is not an easy task! The noisy problems still call to us; the worries stir up a racket in the background! But when we center our minds on the One in control, He gives perfect peace.

Dear Lord, I cannot turn away from the worrisome distractions of my life without Your help. but today, please direct my focus to You and provide for me Your perfect peace.

Peace does not dwell in outward things,
but within the soul; we may preserve it in the midst
of the bitterest pain, if our will remains firm and submissive.
Peace in this life springs from acquiescence to,
not in an exemption from, suffering.

FRANCOIS FENELON

In peace I will lie down and sleep,
for you alone, O Lord, will keep me safe.

PSALM 4:8 NLT

Everywhere

He said, "My presence shall go with you, and I will give you rest."

EXODUS 33:14 NIV

My cat was lost.

The realization hit me late at night. For hours, I called for him, scanning the dark streets of my neighborhood for his black-and-white coat.

Exhausted, I returned home and fell on the couch, weeping. Although I had been praying constantly, I craved my mother's voice most of all. At two in the morning, I dialed her number. Her soft voice calmed my pounding heart and cleared my mind. Minutes later, I found my cat on the front porch.

Hearing my mom's voice on the line was comforting because it was real, tangible. But God is always there too. Just as we get to know our friends better with each passing year, we learn more of God's loving character on every page of the Bible.

His Spirit is in the laughter of a child and the smile of an elderly neighbor. His power is in the stars shining on a summer night and the colors of autumn leaves. At any hour, He's available, expecting your call.

God is all around, hoping to be your comforter and confidant. Do you see Him?

Father, help me to see Your loving presence
everywhere, even in everyday things.

Joy is the settled assurance that God is in control of all
the details of my life, the quiet confidence that ultimately
everything is going to be all right, and the determined
choice to praise God in all things.

KAY WARREN

The eyes of the Lord range throughout
the earth to strengthen those
whose hearts are fully committed to him.

2 CHRONICLES 16:9 NIV

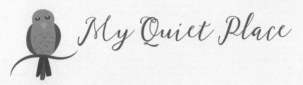

My Quiet Place

Jesus often withdrew to lonely places and prayed.

LUKE 5:16 NIV

When my son and I moved, we left our home, church, friends, and everything familiar. I underestimated the impact of giving up my home office, which had been my work area for freelancing and my place to meet with God. We'd moved in with my parents, so privacy was almost impossible to find. I longed for a special spot for prayer, reflection, or to pray over the phone with a friend without anyone overhearing.

I found the perfect haven while taking a walk—a bench that was just secluded enough to feel like a secret getaway. That became my place to escape to when I needed a moment alone with God to cry out to or thank Him, to rest my mind after a stressful day, or to connect with a prayer partner. Every walk that includes a stop at the bench—even for only a moment—calms me in a unique way.

Jesus needed "lonely places" to meet with His heavenly Father, and so do we. They can be hard to find, but when we find one, it becomes sacred. Where is your quiet place? When is the last time you spent a few precious minutes there?

*Lord, provide the private moments
that I need with You today.*

Draw near to God and He will draw near to you.

JAMES 4:8 NKJV

*Prayer, when we are faithful to it and practice it
at regular times, slowly leads us to an experience
of rest and opens us to God's active presence.*

HENRI NOUWEN

*After he had dismissed the crowds, he went
up on the mountain by himself to pray.*

MATTHEW 14:23 ESV

Finding Jesus

*Jesus said to them, "Why were you looking for me?
Didn't you know that I must be in my Father's house?"*

Luke 2:49 CEB

When Jesus was prepubescent, He and His family traveled to Jerusalem for the Passover festival. Afterward, Mary and Joseph began the ninety-mile trek back home, accompanied by throngs of family members, friends, and others en route. Toward the end of the first day's journey, Mary realized that Jesus wasn't with them.

Talk about a scene right out of *Home Alone.*

So Mary and Joseph made the day trip back into Jerusalem, and after searching for three more days, they found Him in the Temple with the religious leaders. Mary immediately chastised Him, then Jesus answered, "Where did you think I'd be? This is My father's house."

Sometimes I'm like Mary: I think I've lost Jesus. I get so overwhelmed with all the stuff of life, and once I finally think about Him, I look around, asking, "Where'd He go?" Then I make my trip back to find Him.

When you feel lost and alone, know that you will find Jesus right where He's always been. Go there.

God, You calm my fears and cover my mistakes when I feel like I've lost You. Remind me that You were, are, and always will be with me even then. Amen.

Before me, even as behind, God is, and all is well.

JOHN GREENLEAF WHITTIER

God has said, "Never will I leave you; never will I forsake you." So we say with confidence, "The Lord is my helper; I will not be afraid. What can mere mortals do to me?"

HEBREWS 13:5–6 NIV

Cast your burden on the Lord,
and he will sustain you;
he will never permit
the righteous to be moved.

PSALM 55:22 ESV

Pick-Your-Own Produce Farms

Let the peace of Christ rule in your hearts.

COLOSSIANS 3:15 NASB

Have you ever visited a "pick-your-own" farm? Eager customers enter the garden, pick the fruits or vegetables they would like to purchase, and proudly take their harvest home.

What makes this chore appeal to people who could buy fresh produce elsewhere without physical labor? Maybe the allure is due to the benefit of pausing from daily chores, thus providing an opportunity to take a deep breath and relax a bit. Furthermore, glimpsing the countryside beauty of white fluffy clouds, majestic oaks, and green pastures reminds us of God's power and creativity. Concerns seem to vanish in this setting.

When we're tired, frustrated, or fearful, inhaling outdoor air slowly produces calmness. Gazing up at a clear blue sky often reminds us that the Creator of the earth is also our loving heavenly Father. This thought alone minimizes problems. Nothing overwhelms Him. No challenge is too great for Him to solve. No concern is too small to mention in prayer. When we're fatigued, doubtful, or discouraged, a brief walk or drive to a rural area can inspire us to take a deep breath and enjoy peace as only He can give.

*Lord Jesus, call me to rest my mind
and body and to allow Your peace
to calm and govern my heart.*

The Lord is my shepherd, I lack nothing.
He makes me lie down in green pastures,
he leads me beside quiet waters, he refreshes my soul.

PSALM 23:1–2 NIV

*Fair are the meadows, fairer still the woodlands,
robed in the blooming garb of spring:
Jesus is fairer, Jesus is purer
who makes the woeful heart to sing.*

MUNSTER GESANGBUCH

Choose Faith over Fear

You drew near on the day I called on you,
and said, "Do not fear!"

LAMENTATIONS 3:57 NKJV

Last year began with a huge test of my faith and trust. I couldn't show my fears and anxieties, as I had others depending on me to be strong and calm. Outwardly, I looked fine. My mind, however, was firing on *all* cylinders with "what if" thoughts. I had to learn, quickly, to call on and cast my cares on God, or else I was going to find myself sinking in my fears. At that moment, my fears certainly felt bigger than my faith. God placed others—nurses, friends, and family—in my path to remind me that peace of mind was just a (prayer) call away.

It is not possible to focus on worry and prayer at the same time. Things beyond our control can be frightening. However, being fearful does not mean a lack of faith. Even Jesus was fearful at times (Mark 14:33). You do not have to let fear stop you from taking a deep breath and a step of faith into God's waiting arms. He wants to give you rest. All you have to do is call on Him.

Lord, in exchange for my fears, I will choose faith instead of anticipating the worst because I know You are in control. Amen.

Our lives are full of supposes. Suppose this should happen,
or suppose that should happen; what could we do;
how could we bear it? But, if we are living in the high tower
of the dwelling place of God, all these supposes will drop out
of our lives. We shall be quiet from the fear of evil, for no
threatenings of evil can penetrate into the high tower of God.

HANNAH WHITALL SMITH

"Fear not…. I will help you," says the Lord and your Redeemer, the Holy One of Israel.

ISAIAH 41:14 NKJV

A Troubled Heart

Don't let your hearts be troubled. Trust in God, and trust also in me.

JOHN 14:1 NLT

There is something about a walk on the beach that will clear your mind and quiet your heart. When I lived in Florida, I often took long walks on the beach. Meandering beyond the crowd, I'd plop down on the wet sand and stare at the ocean.

Waves crashed against sandy shores. Seagulls glided through clear skies. Occasionally, a dolphin stuck his fin through swirling waters. His bottle-like nose and glassy eye seemed to smile as he splashed the air.

Breathtaking.

As I sat, I'd sing. Praise would erupt from my soul and disappear behind me into the strong wind. No one heard me. I could barely hear. But God did.

After singing, I would pray. Pouring out my requests to the Lord, I felt my heart lighten. Knowing that I have a Father who hears me in a strong wind on a sandy beach always calmed my troubled heart.

After an hour or so, I would walk home sloshing feet through a foamy shore while gazing at coquina shells pushing up for a breath.

Maybe you have a troubled heart today. Let me give you a prescription—get alone with God. Seek His face. Praise and pray.

And, it's free.

Lord, thank You for
calming my troubled heart.

Let the first act when waking be to place yourself, your heart, mind, faculties, your whole being, in God's hands. Ask Him to take entire possession of you, to be the guide of your soul, your life, your wisdom, your strength. He wants us to seek Him in all our needs, that we may both know Him truly, and draw closer and closer to Him; and in prayer we gain an invisible force which will triumph over seemingly hopeless difficulties.

H. L. SIDNEY LEAR

I am always with you; you hold me by my right hand.

PSALM 73:23 NIV

Speak, move, act in peace, as if you were in
prayer. In truth, this is prayer.

FRANCOIS FENELON

Hope for the Future

*I know the plans I have for you, declares the Lord,
plans for welfare and not for evil, to give you a future and a hope.*

JEREMIAH 29:11 ESV

When the world presses in and our lives seem to be in total chaos, remembering God's love can be difficult. The more stressed and fearful we become, the more the temptation to seek answers in other places can feel like a craving hunger. We want help and answers.

But no one knows us the way God does. He has known us—and His plans for us—from the time of our conception (Jeremiah 1:5). Even when we don't know our own minds, He does. His designs for us are never against us. He sees "the big picture," and His love and mercy will bring good in our lives, no matter how rough the journey is at this moment. He wants peace for us, and hope for our future.

God does not forget about us, and His mercy and kindness continually surround us, even when it feels like life is completely out of control. When we remember that, when we rely on that, we can find that a calm peace will settle on us.

Lord, when life delivers chaos into our lives, help us remember that You only desire good for us. When we trust in You, we can have hope for our future. Amen.

I knew you before I formed you in your mother's womb. Before you were born I set you apart.

JEREMIAH 1:5 NLT

Ah, Hope! what would life be, stripped of your encouraging smiles, that teach us to look behind the dark clouds of today, for the golden beams that are to gild the morrow.

SUSANNA MOODIE

God Has Supernatural Peace for You

May the Lord of peace himself always give you his peace no matter what happens. The Lord be with you all.

2 THESSALONIANS 3:16 NLT

It never failed. When my daughters were young, they were very afraid of storms. With the first boom of thunder, Abby and Allyson were crawling into bed with us. I could totally relate because I was also afraid of storms when I was a little girl. I can remember pulling the covers over my head and praying, "God, please make the storm go away!"

Today I find myself praying that same prayer when the storms of life get too scary. And just when I think I can't handle one more black cloud, God reminds me that He is with me, that He is my covering, and that He has supernatural peace available to me no matter what is happening around me.

God is with you, too. He doesn't always calm the storms in the way that we desire or anticipate, but He will be with you throughout every storm and love you through it. Why not come out from under the covers of life and call on the One who is able to calm all the storms?

Father, thank You for Your
supernatural peace, and thank You
for never leaving me. Amen.

As you walk through the valley of the unknown, you will find
the footprints of Jesus both in front of you and beside you.

CHARLES STANLEY

You have been a refuge for the poor,
a refuge for the needy in their distress,
a shelter from the storm and a shade from the heat.

ISAIAH 25:4 NIV

Sometimes God allows what He hates
to accomplish what He loves.

JONI EARECKSON TADA

Just Pray

Be anxious for nothing, but in everything
by prayer and supplication with thanksgiving
let your requests be made known to God.

PHILIPPIANS 4:6 NASB

My son Noah won a national storytelling competition, requiring us to fly to Utah for the award ceremony. We had never flown before, and Noah was terrified. A friend drove us to the airport, and as we got closer, Noah panicked. Unbeknownst to me, he posted his fears on social media and texted his mother, requesting prayer.

On the boarding passes I noticed our seats were separate for the initial leg of the trip, so, at the last minute, I changed our flight so we could sit together. We boarded a connector scheduled to last an hour, found our seats, and, surprisingly, Noah insisted on sitting next to the window. As we took off, I prayed for the Lord to calm his nerves; my wife and others were praying the same way back home. Soon after takeoff, a flight attendant gave us snacks and drinks. We landed and prepared for another flight to Salt Lake City.

I asked Noah how he was feeling. "Great!" he replied heartily. "Flying is the ONLY way to travel!" The rest of our trip went smoothly, with no nerves. Jesus heard those prayers and answered mightily. He was with us all the way, calming a young boy—and his father.

Lord, thank You for the prayers of loved ones. Calm our fears as we lean on You.

This is the confidence that we have in Him,
that if we ask anything according to His will, He hears us.

1 JOHN 5:14 NKJV

A true faith must rest solidly on God's character and His Word,
not on our particular conceptions of what He ought to do.

ELISABETH ELLIOT

We shall steer safely through every storm,
so long as our heart is right,
our intention fervent. our courage steadfast,
and our trust fixed on God.

ST. FRANCIS DE SALES

The Art of Giving Up

The Lord himself will fight for you. Just stay calm.

EXODUS 14:14 NLT

I watch him try and shove his foot into the shoe, growing more frustrated each second. I could step in, but I choose to wait. I know I can't teach my son anything until he's ready to learn.

Finally, I hear those magic words, "Mom, can you help?"

In similar fashion, God often waits for us to ask Him, to demonstrate our reliance on Him. He longs for us to depend on Him and give up trying to live life on our own. After all, God gives His grace to the weak ones who ask, not the religious strength trainers.

This isn't giving up in defeat, but surrendering to God as the Israelites learned to do in the wilderness. God wants to fight for us, but first we need to be still. God longs to help us in every situation, if we'll only wait and rest in Him. So often we muddle through each day on our own when infinite grace awaits us.

Waiting on God is difficult, but it's much easier than plowing through our days without God's grace.

Father, we surrender to You today;
as we rest and wait on You,
please pour Your grace over our lives.

God always has and always will look for men and women
who say to Him, "I trust you so much, I'm all in.
I want your way not mine. I am willing to live by faith!"

CHIP INGRAM

The Lord your God, who goes before you,
He will fight for you.

DEUTERONOMY 1:30 NKJV

# Enjoy the Quiet

All the lands are at rest and at peace; they break into singing.

Isaiah 14:7 NIV

After every storm in life, a kind of calm descends. This happens in the most mundane ways, like when you experience that deafening calm after the baby goes to sleep. This vacuum occurs at more poignant moments too, like when the house becomes eerily quiet after the last teenager moves out. Whatever the tsunami—an illness, a heartbreak, a job loss—it will be followed by a calm, an emptiness, a dead space.

Your temptation will be to fill in that space with more activity. You'll go looking for something—noise, commotion, relationships, anything to fill the void. You'll volunteer for one more job at church or get coffee with one more acquaintance or take on more hours at work or start some new venture.

Don't. Be still for just a moment. Enjoy this quiet while it lasts.

There's nothing wrong with this space. It's not empty; it's filled with silence. It's not wasted; it's restful. Soon enough you can add back all those good activities—if you still want to.

For now, put on another pot of tea, go to your favorite chair, and just enjoy the quiet. This, too, is a gift from God.

Lord, lead me to rest before
the next storm comes.

If the Lord Jehovah makes us wait, let us do so
with our whole hearts; for blessed are all they that wait
for Him. He is worth waiting for. The waiting itself
is beneficial to us: it tries faith, exercises patience,
trains submission, and endears the blessing when it comes.
The Lord's people have always been a waiting people.

CHARLES SPURGEON

I wait for the Lord, my soul waits,
and in his word I hope;
my soul waits for the Lord
more than watchmen for the morning,

PSALM 130:5–6 ESV

Peace, Be Still

He arose and rebuked the wind, and said unto the sea, Peace,
be still. And the wind ceased, and there was a great calm.

MARK 4:39 ESV

Somehow the picture of the disciples at night in the middle of a raging storm helps me. The rain was pouring down, the lightning was flashing, the wind was gusting, the waves were tossing, and Jesus was sleeping. They could watch His chest rise and fall with deep breathing. They were physically in His presence in their little boat. And still they were overcome with fear and desperate for His help.

When my life's storms feel out of control and Jesus seems to be a bit slow in rushing to my rescue, I like to share the disciples' company. I may not be able to see Him, but I can read in His Word the sure promises that He is with me, that He will never leave me. But still the rain pounds down and I am afraid.

Still He sleeps. My boat takes on water. I'm pleading for help. At last, Jesus speaks. "Peace, be still." But is He talking to the storm or to me? At His word, the winds and waves obey Him. Do I?

*Jesus, when I cry out because of the storm,
help me to remember that You are with me
and You are still in control.*

When I cannot understand my Father's leading,
And it seems to be but hard and cruel fate,
Still I hear that gentle whisper ever pleading,
God is working, God is faithful, ONLY WAIT.

LETTIE B. COWMAN

*He stilled the storm to a whisper;
the waves of the sea were hushed.*

PSALM 107:29 NIV

Praying Peace for Others

The Lord lift up his countenance upon you
and give you peace.

NUMBERS 6:26 ESV

Prayers of blessing can be found throughout the Old Testament. A spoken blessing is a positive Biblical statement over our friends and family and can be such a beautiful gift to them. Asking for God's blessing upon others is an act of giving of ourselves and a level of care that we express with words rooted in divine intervention. What an expression of hope for others when we pray for their peace. In a chaotic world, we can bless others with a prayer for calm. In a world full of anxious people, we can pray for their peace.

Yet I'm afraid my prayer time can often be consumed with a list of petitions. This list is extensive as many of my friends and family have great needs. Our churches, communities, and even our nation must be prayed over, and yet as I pray for this list of petitions, I realize this passage is urging us to do more than make petition for others and their needs.

We all crave peace in our souls. Our comfort, joy, and peace are found in the heart of God, and we should want others to know this joy and ultimately this peace.

*Heavenly Father, we praise You
for being the Prince of Peace.*

I wish you humor and a twinkle in the eye. I wish you glory
and the strength to bear its burdens. I wish you sunshine
on your path and storms to season your journey. I wish you
peace—in the world in which you live and in the smallest
corner of the heart where truth is kept. I wish you faith—
to help define your living and your life. More I cannot wish
you—except perhaps love—to make all the rest worthwhile.

ROBERT A. WARD

*I thank my God upon every remembrance
of you, always in every prayer of mine
making request for you all with joy…being
confident of this very thing, that He who
has begun a good work in you will complete
it until the day of Jesus Christ.*

PHILIPPIANS 1:2–6 NKJV

Strength in Sitting Still

Wait patiently for the Lord. Be brave and courageous.
Yes, wait patiently for the Lord.

PSALM 27:14 NLT

Why are we afraid of staying still—of doing absolutely nothing—as if our lives depended on motion to keep us steady and strong? The more we do, the better we feel; the slower the pace, the more we panic. Today we go-go-go 24/7 with iPhone in hand and a schedule packed with a thousand things. But if it should stop, anxiety suddenly fills us with that helpless, sinking feeling.

Strength has nothing to do with action, just as stillness is not inherently lazy. There is nothing weak about waiting, especially in times of confusion and doubt. It takes great self-control to sit perfectly still, but it's in our stillness that God is able to do His finest work.

As one wheat kernel is planted in the ground and dies (John 12:24), it gives birth to one hundred more at harvest time. By sitting quietly, waiting for God's divine direction, our spiritual muscles double. Yes, it's the toughest thing to do—sitting still—but it is through strength in stillness that heaven is opened and angels are dispatched. *Wait and see!*

Jesus, mute the inner alarms, calm my racing heart, and comfort my fears that come with inaction. Remind me that in being still, You have complete control. Amen.

As a child of God, how much more do we need times of complete solitude—times to deal with the spiritual realities of life and to be alone with God the Father. If there was ever anyone who could dispense with special times of solitude and fellowship, it was our Lord. Yet even He could not maintain His full strength and power for His work and His fellowship with the Father without His quiet time. God desires that every servant of His would understand and perform this blessed practice, that His church would know how to train its children to recognize this high and holy privilege, and that every believer would realize the importance of making time for God alone.

LETTIE B. COWMAN

Be strong, and let your heart take courage, all you who wait for the Lord!

Trusting God When Things Are Good

The Lord is good to all; he has compassion on all he has made.

PSALM 145:9 NIV

Sometimes life is going incredibly well. You don't have a care in the world because everything is "coming up roses." But then anxiety starts creeping in. You think that life can't possibly be this good and you begin to fear that soon life will get turned upside down. You don't know where or when it's coming, but it must be coming. Isn't that how the world works?

When life is good and you're still experiencing anxiety, sometimes the best thing you can do is just breathe and be mindful of the moment. Remind yourself of the great God you serve. Our God is a good, good Father. He loves His children. He wants you to live an abundant life full of blessing. Then allow the negative feelings to pass as you rest in God's faithful, loving arms.

He does not give and take away peace, as the world does. He just keeps giving out unending peace. Therefore, we don't need to let our hearts be troubled. We can trust in Him.

Dear God, thank You for
Your everlasting peace. We trust in You
always, in good times and bad.

Oh, how great is the goodness of God, greater than
we can understand. There are moments and there
are mysteries of the divine mercy over which the heavens
are astounded. Let our judgment of souls cease,
for God's mercy upon them is extraordinary.

MARY FAUSTINA KOWALSKA

How great is your goodness, which you
have stored up for those who fear you,
which you bestow in the sight of men
on those who take refuge in you.

PSALM 31:19 NIV

God Joins Us in Our Trouble

"Take heart; it is I. Do not be afraid."
And he got into the boat with them, and the wind ceased.
And they were utterly astounded.

MARK 6:49–51 ESV

Lately, my nonfiction reading has had a recurring theme of friendship during difficult illnesses like cancer. Many of us struggle with finding the right words to say in these times. A common thread from these writers is to be willing to just show up and sit with our friends through their difficulty. Having the "right words" is not necessary.

As I read this passage, I thought of the encouraging words from these authors and how similar these ideas are. Here in the midst of the disciples' terrifying circumstances, Jesus got in the boat with them and joined them in the middle of their crisis. While the winds calmed and the angry seas ceased to roar in these verses, we see that even if the storm had not stopped, Jesus was still sitting with them in the middle of that terrifying time. What comfort for us that no matter what storm we face, the God of glory, Jesus the precious Son of God, joins us right in the middle of our mess. Peace in the midst of our storms.

*We thank You, Lord, for the comfort
it is to know You join us
in the middle of our trials.*

When I cannot feel the faith of assurance,
I live by the fact of God's faithfulness.

MATTHEW HENRY

Let not your heart be troubled;
you believe in God, believe also in Me.

JOHN 14:1 NKJV

*There is never a moment when God is not
in control. Relax! He's got you covered.*

MANDY HALE

In any trial, in any bitter situation, you are not alone, you are not helpless, you are not a victim. You have a tree, a cross, shown to you by the Sovereign God of Calvary. Whatever the trial or temptation, it is not more than you can bear. It is bearable. It can be handled.

KAY ARTHUR

Breathe... Even in the Midst of Chaos

Cast all your anxiety on him because he cares for you.

1 PETER 5:7 NIV

Peace. Rest. What do these look like to you? Are they things you can easily visualize, or are they impossible for you to even imagine? Did you ever wonder why that was the case?

Growing up, I always loved the peaceful feeling I felt during a summer storm. However, I have found that I am unable to experience that same peace during the storms of life. You often hear people say things like, "Oh, she doesn't have a care in the world!" Well, that is highly unlikely. Everyone encounters worry of *some* sort.

Today's verse is a popular one, and many people memorize it...for good reason. There is something calming about knowing that we can trust God to deal with things. Worry is counterproductive. It takes away that sense of peace God wants us to have, despite our circumstances. In the Bible, Paul presents prayer as an alternative option to worry, one that will give us a peace beyond any normal comprehension (Philippians 4:4–7). Focusing on God's Word will allow your heart and mind to be filled with the expectancy of God's promises.

*Lord, while I may not always know
what to do, I know I can never go wrong
in casting my cares on You. Amen.*

It is not the cares of today, but the cares of tomorrow,
that weigh a man down. For the needs of today
we have corresponding strength given. For the morrow
we are told to trust. It is not ours yet. It is when
tomorrow's burden is added to the burden of today
that the weight is more than a man can bear.

GEORGE MACDONALD

*Whenever I am afraid, I will trust in You.
In God (I will praise His word),
in God I have put my trust; I will not fear.*

PSALM 56:3–4 NKJV

Peace Isn't
the Absence of Stress

The Lord blesses his people with peace.

PSALM 29:11 NIV

I used to have a narrow view of the word peace. It always brought to mind calm settings, perfectly clean houses, and relationships without conflict. For me, peace was a bubble that burst anytime my stress level increased.

It's hard to live like that though. It leads to all kinds of false expectations, especially in light of how many times God promises us peace. So I began to dig in and search out what it means to have God's peace.

I discovered it's more powerful than anything I imagined, and it goes beyond just the absence of stress. It comes when I focus on God, instead of my situation. I found that when I draw closer to God, He gives me peace that flows through any circumstances I'm facing. For me, God's peace is the certainty that He's in control and that no matter the difficulties, something better lies ahead.

Dear Lord, don't ever let me try
to live without Your peace
flowing through my life. Amen.

Grace and peace be yours in abundance
through the knowledge of God and of Jesus our Lord.

2 PETER 1:2 NIV

In all my perplexities and distresses,
the Bible has never failed to give me light and strength.

ROBERT E. LEE

Sometimes the Lord calms the storm.
Sometimes He lets the storm rage
and calms His child.

Waiting without Worry

He said to his servant, "Go up now, look toward the sea."
So he went up and looked and said, "There is nothing."
And he said, "Go back" seven times. It came about
at the seventh time, that he said, "Behold, a cloud as small
as a man's hand is coming up from the sea."

1 KINGS 18:43–44 NASB

Pray. Wait. Repeat. Elijah's first six attempts petitioning provision end in disappointment.

After each *no* Elijah calmly continues praying. He doesn't give up, nor does he strive to put some sort of alternate plan into action. He expectantly returns again and again, and rejoices over what appears to be a meager response to his prayers.

Elijah has witnessed God's faithfulness in the past and trusts God is still faithful, even in the midst of momentary disappointment.

Do you find yourself in a similar season of asking and waiting? Instead of getting worked up and worried over an uncontrollable future, we can use our waiting as an opportunity to let go of our timelines. To take a deep breath. To allow our anxious hearts to find peace in God's perfect timing. We can trust, like Elijah did, that *no* right now doesn't mean *no* forever.

Faithful God, give me peace while I wait.
Help me trade anxiety for trust; You will
do what is best at the right time.

Restlessness and impatience change nothing except
our peace and joy. Peace does not dwell in outward things,
but in the heart prepared to wait trustfully and quietly
on Him who has all things safely in His hands.

ELISABETH ELLIOT

Therefore the Lord will wait, that He may
be gracious to you; and therefore He will be
exalted, that He may have mercy on you....
Blessed are all those who wait for Him.

ISAIAH 30:18 NKJV

Stopped in My Tracks

Be still, and know that I am God.

PSALM 46:10 ESV

Too much to do, too many commitments, too many times I should have said no. Taking on more than I can realistically accomplish is something I'm guilty of from time to time, leaving me exhausted and flustered.

Recently I did it again. I agreed to host a gathering of approximately twenty people. Not only was I furnishing the meal, but I also volunteered to give a ten-minute devotion. A friend said she would help set up and serve the meal.

Two days before my friend was to help me, she became ill, requiring a short stay in the hospital. Then on the day of the event, a last-minute meeting required my presence in a city more than two hours away. The meeting was scheduled for 9:00 a.m. and, if nothing unusual happened, I'd be back home by midafternoon. The meal was scheduled for 5:00 p.m. Needless to say, my level of anxiety rose.

"Help me, Lord," I prayed. "Give me a calm spirit." As I stopped for a moment and gave thanks for His faithfulness, I heard Him answer me, *Be still and know that I am God*, and I breathed in His peaceful confidence.

*Lord, help me to daily breathe
Your peace and stillness.*

Knowing that God is faithful, it really helps me to not be captivated by worry. But knowing that He will do what He has said, He will cause it to happen, whatever He has promised, and then it causes me to be less involved in worrying about a situation.

JOSH McDOWELL

*I wait quietly before God,
for my victory comes from him.*

PSALM 62:1 NLT

Enjoy the Journey!

Rejoice in the Lord always. I will say it again: Rejoice!

Philippians 4:4 niv

Before I had a book published, I truly thought that I'd be forever happy once I saw one of my books on the shelves of a bookstore. And, I'll be honest—it was pretty exciting the first time I found my book at our local Barnes & Noble. (I took a picture next to it, giving the "thumbs up" sign. No shame.) It was even more thrilling when I did my first book signing! But, you know what? That happiness was fleeting. After a few months, I began worrying about my next book contract. I worried I might be a "one book wonder." I worried that my book wouldn't sell very many copies. I worried and worried and worried, and that worry eventually turned into fear and unhappiness.

The truth is, if you're not happy and at peace when you don't have any books on the shelves of Barnes & Noble, you won't be happy when you have twenty-five books on their shelves, or even seventy! We have to determine in our hearts to enjoy the journey on the way to where God is taking us, and celebrate those milestones along the way. Choose joy today!

*Father, help me to enjoy the journey
You're taking me on and appreciate
every blessing along the way. Amen.*

Love, consolation, and peace bloom
only in the garden of sweet contentment.

MARTHA ANDERSON

I have learned in whatever situation I am to be content.
I know how to be brought low, and I know how to abound.
In any and every circumstance, I have learned the secret
of facing plenty and hunger, abundance and need.
I can do all things through him who strengthens me.

PHILIPPIANS 4:11–13 ESV

*Concentrate on counting your blessings and
you'll have little time to count anything else.*

WOODROW KROLL

Looking Up, Instead of In

*Letting your sinful nature control your mind leads to death.
But letting the Spirit control your mind leads to life
and peace. For the sinful nature is always hostile to God.*

Romans 8:6–7 nlt

Has your mind ever been stuck on a merry-go-round, where contemplation slips into harmful navel-gazing? Constantly looking inward can deepen stress and become the breeding ground of anxiety.

Helen Keller found a joyful antidote in self-forgetfulness. She describes it well. "I try to make the light in others' eyes my sun, the music in others' ears my symphony, the smile on others' lips my happiness."

The gospel, too, rings of this kind of selfless love, and Jesus urged us to follow Him in washing feet and rescuing the poor and wounded. Serving others does help us step off the merry-go-round. Turning our gaze to God, however, pulls the plug on the carnival ride altogether.

Take a moment today to look up instead of in. Set your gaze on the One who never takes His eyes off you. The God who beckons you to cast your cares on Him longs to unburden you and bring you into a spacious place of worship.

Lord Jesus, when our gaze gravitates
inward, help us reposition our focus
upward and outward.

Turn your eyes upon Jesus,
Look full in His wonderful face;
And the things of earth will grow strangely dim
In the light of His glory and grace.

HELEN HOWARTH LEMMEL

Let us run with endurance the race God has set before us.
We do this by keeping our eyes on Jesus, the champion who
initiates and perfects our faith.

HEBREWS 12:1–2 NLT

I'm a little pencil in the hand of a writing
God, who is sending a love letter to the world.

MOTHER TERESA

The Overwhelming Life

From the ends of the earth, I cry to you for help when my heart is overwhelmed. Lead me to the towering rock of safety, for you are my safe refuge.

PSALM 61:2–3 NLT

Feeling crushed by responsibilities and duties is common to most of us. The pressures of work, family, church, and other commitments weigh down on us, threating to overwhelm us. When we look at all we have to take care of, a sense of panic sets in, making us desire nothing more than a long nap and a chair on a beach. Yet finding time to breathe, to find a few moments of peace, feels impossible. There's just too much to do!

These are the times that turning to God for help is more important than ever. In Him who is our refuge, we can find a clear path. He will provide the peace, the hope, and the guidance to get through each task one-by-one and to maintain our sense of calm direction.

By focusing on Him, we gain perspective. As we remember what's important to Him, we can prioritize with more clarity...and we may even learn to say no more often, whenever someone starts a sentence, "Can you—?"

Lord, help us turn to You when we are
overwhelmed. Grant us a sense of peace,
an open heart, and a clear vision
to deal with all we've been handed.
You are our only refuge. Amen.

My God is my rock, in whom I take refuge,
my shield and the horn of my salvation.
He is my stronghold, my refuge and my savior.

2 SAMUEL 22:3 NIV

Learn to say "no" to the good
so you can say "yes" to the best.

JOHN C. MAXWELL

The Queen of Chaos

God is not the author of confusion, but of peace.

1 CORINTHIANS 14:33 KJV

I don't like mess or chaos. That's ironic since my life is filled with those things. Some days my to-do list is so long that I'm sure it must stretch to Kansas. And I've found it doesn't help when I add a major remodeling project to the mix, one that somehow ends up in every room with saws grinding, hammers pounding, and workmen coming in and out. And then there's the sheetrock dust, ladders, boards, buckets, and tools all over the house. Yes folks, total chaos.

But then I realized something that helped me. I cleaned one room that wasn't having much work done in it, a room that was somewhat away from the mayhem. When I needed to write or when the chaos in the rest of the house started driving me crazy, I could go to that quiet, restful place and feel an instant peace.

The same is true spiritually. When life starts getting me down, when the chaos of my to-do list starts overwhelming me, I can go to my quiet place, to the God who is the author of peace, and I can find rest for my soul.

*Father, remind me that true rest
is found in You. Amen.*

The moment you wake up each morning,
all your wishes and hopes for the day rush at you
like wild animals. And the first job each morning
consists in shoving it all back; in listening to that other voice,
taking that other point of view, letting that other,
larger, stronger, quieter life come flowing in.

C. S. LEWIS

*Learning to be quiet before the Lord
is one of the greatest challenges we face
today in our quest to enter in
and experience true intimacy with Him.*

JAMES GOLL

 *Contentment*

Godliness with contentment is great gain. For we brought nothing into the world, and we can take nothing out of it.

1 TIMOTHY 6:6–7 NIV

One summer evening, my husband and I took a walk through our neighborhood, holding hands. Our lives were a bit of a mess at that moment. He was having migraines and couldn't help around the house. I wasn't feeling well, either. Because money was tight, each bill that we paid was painful.

Then we started talking about how we don't need all the "extra" stuff our neighbors had. He gripped my hand my tightly, saying, "*This* is what we need." We had love, a home, and our faith. That was enough.

When we desire the wrong things, we're left disappointed and restless. We can forget our worldly wish list by shifting our cravings to God—knowing Him, loving Him, and using the gifts He's given us.

None of us have everything. Rather than feeling sorry for ourselves, we can find peaceful contentment by counting the blessings we do have. God is the greatest one of all, and He's the only One that satisfies.

*Father, remove my desires for earthly things,
like possessions and recognition, and replace
them with yearnings to know You.*

Do not worry about your life, what you will eat
or what you will drink; nor about your body,
what you will put on.... Your heavenly Father knows
that you need all these things. But seek first
the kingdom of God and His righteousness,
and all these things shall be added to you.

MATTHEW 6:25, 32–33 NKJV

*We would worry less if we praised more.
Thanksgiving is the enemy
of discontent and dissatisfaction.*

HARRY IRONSIDE

Peace in Uncertainty

Peace I leave with you; my peace I give you.
I do not give to you as the world gives.
Do not let your hearts be troubled and do not be afraid.

JOHN 14:27 NIV

There I was, driving down the highway, staring at the back of the big moving truck in front of me, wondering how this would work out. The job had fallen through and our future was unknown.

All I could do was pray. Prayer put peace in my heart, a peace that only my heavenly Father could give. A peace that would stand firmly in my heart as each month passed and no job had been found. A peace that kept my soul joyful and my marriage intact. A peace that kept me focused on Him and His great love.

During that time the words of Isaiah 26:3 came to life in me: "He will keep him in perfect peace whose mind is stayed on Him." Planted deep in my soul, that perfect peace given freely by God was all I needed to see that journey through.

Father God, when circumstances bring
feelings of anxiety help me to stay focused
on Your peace, which only You can give,
so that my heart is free to love and my soul
is full in Your presence. In Jesus's name, amen.

God is in control, and therefore in EVERYTHING
I can give thanks—not because of the situation but because
of the One who directs and rules over it.

KAY ARTHUR

Those who know your name
trust in you, for you, Lord,
have never forsaken those who seek you.

PSALM 9:10 NIV

Giving It to God

*Humble yourselves, therefore, under God's mighty hand,
that he may lift you up in due time. Cast all your anxiety
on him because he cares for you.*

1 PETER 5:6–7 NIV

"I did it my way." These words were made famous
by Frank Sinatra in 1969. They ring true in the hearts of
millions each day as we face struggles. We see a certain
strength in doing things our way. If we make it through our
way, then we can tell everyone we did it on our own. We
lie to ourselves, telling ourselves that by doing so we are
strong. True strength, however, is found in humility.

When we do things our way, the struggle is intense and
unbearable, yet when we humble ourselves under God's
loving hands, the struggle may remain but peace replaces
anxiety and fear. The struggle becomes bearable.

Giving our worries, fears, and circumstances to God
takes faith and strength. We have to trust that His way is
the better way. One thing is assured, we will never regret
saying "I did it His way."

Father God, I want to live my life Your way. Show me the areas in my life I have not given up to You. Give me the strength to let go and let You work in my life. In Jesus's name, amen.

I am the vine, you are the branches.
He who abides in Me, and I in him, bears much fruit;
for without Me you can do nothing.

JOHN 15:5 NKJV

It is not my ability, but my response to God's ability that counts.

CORRIE TEN BOOM

The Perfect Storm

When anxiety was great within me,
your consolation brought me joy.

PSALM 94:19 NIV

The busier our lives become, the more out of control our thoughts and worries can be. As we rush from one task to another, concerns about our families, our work, our communities abound. Thoughts swirl about in our minds, unfocused and jumbled, stirring up our worries and anxieties like a great wind.

This struggle isn't new. Psalm 39 describes the struggle to control our words and thoughts, how the storms of emotion can overwhelm us. The whirl of thoughts is the very enemy of peace, an obstacle to trusting God with every aspect of our lives. Jesus also cautioned us about giving in to worry (Matthew 6:25–34).

Surrendering our worries to God isn't always easy. Some of us have to start over every day! But Psalm 94 is a reminder that we can indeed relinquish our anxieties to God, rely on Him, and take comfort in His promises. He offers consolation in all things.

Take a deep breath and say a quick prayer to give your cares to God and ask for His peace. He will deliver.

Lord, I offer up to You all my worries. Lift them from my heart and grant me Your peace. I know Your care for me will prevail. Amen.

In the secret of God's tabernacle no enemy can find us, and no troubles can reach us.... The secret of His presence is a more secure refuge than a thousand Gibraltars. I do not mean that no trials come. They may come in abundance, but they cannot penetrate into the sanctuary of the soul, and we may dwell in perfect peace even in the midst of life fiercest storms.

HANNAH WHITALL SMITH

Lord, where do I put my hope? My only hope is in you.

PSALM 39:7 NLT

Just Whisper His Name

He who searches our hearts knows the mind of the Spirit,
because the Spirit intercedes for the saints
in accordance with God's will.

ROMANS 8:27 NIV

The only way we can pray is with the help of the Holy Spirit, who intercedes for us. Prayer is a process that helps us overcome fear; we can pray without ceasing by being mindful of the presence of God. He has promised us He will never leave us; He's always there.

When we pray, we're conflicted by what we want and by what God wills for us, and we need God's wisdom when we pray and study His Word. The Holy Spirit reminds us of what we have learned, and we're encouraged.

Sometimes we become comfortable in our relationship with God and, without realizing it, we take Him for granted. Then when a crisis comes along and our world turns upside down, we forget God is right here with us. We forget to enter into His presence through prayer and to breathe in His peace and comfort. But by taking a deep breath and whispering the name of Jesus, we remember the benefits of God's presence, and we remember He will never leave us.

God of comfort, bring peace to our
spirits as we face things that
turn our world upside down.

Our Father in heaven, may your name be kept holy.
May your Kingdom come soon.
May your will be done on earth, as it is in heaven.

MATTHEW 6:9–10 NLT

Prayer delights God's ear; it melts
His heart; and opens His hand.
God cannot deny a praying soul.

THOMAS WATSON

I believe God, through His Spirit,
grants us love, joy, and peace
no matter what is happening
in our lives. As Christians,
we shouldn't expect our joy
to always feel like happiness,
but instead recognize joy as inner security—
a safeness in our life with Christ.

JILL BRISCOE

Anxious Toil vs. Rest

It is in vain that you rise up early
and go late to rest, eating the bread of anxious toil;
for he gives to his beloved sleep.

PSALM 127:2 ESV

Approximately one-third of all people will experience insomnia at some point in their lives. Scientists have determined that we need an average of eight hours of sleep each night in order to maintain a healthy lifestyle. When we miss out on the quantity of sleep we need regularly, our physical health declines and many illnesses and diseases can develop. How much of this sleep problem can be traced to another equally insidious problem—anxiety?

The idea of anxiety here is working with a lack of peace. Fear and fretting should not be a part of our labor. There are many side effects of anxiety on our bodies, both mental and physical, and it definitely inhibits our ability to get rest. The Bible teaches us that we are not to be in anxious toil but rather that He gives us rest. If you've ever struggled to get a good night's sleep, then this precious promise should bring such comfort to you. The rest that God gives allows us freedom to work hard and then leave the results in His hands.

*What a comfort to know, dear Father, that
You give to us Your beloved peaceful rest!*

Why are you cast down, O my soul, and why are
you in turmoil within me? Hope in God;
for I shall again praise him, my salvation and my God.

PSALM 43:5 ESV

An unpeaceful mind cannot operate normally.
Hence the Apostle teaches us to "have no anxiety
about anything" (Philippians 4:6). Deliver all
anxious thoughts to God as soon as they arise.
Let the peace of God maintain your heart and mind.

WATCHMAN NEE

*I lie down and sleep; I wake again,
because the Lord sustains me.*

PSALM 3:5 NIV

Stop Asking Questions

He will be called Wonderful Counselor,
Mighty God, Everlasting Father, Prince of Peace.

ISAIAH 9:6 NIV

How many times have you gone on a trip and all you hear is "Are we there yet?" or "Can I have a snack?" Have you ever told a child, "Stop asking so many questions"?

Children will ask all kinds of questions because they are learning new things constantly. Whether you're a parent, teacher, or relative, teaching children is one of the harder things in life. It requires patience to explain things that come naturally to adults.

Sometimes we, too, ask God lots of questions about life situations. When will I get the call for a new job? Who will I marry? When will I start having children?

God wants us, His children, to come with requests and questions about life. He's the Wonderful Counselor who will never tell us to stop asking.

Depend on Him for the answers you're struggling with today. If we simply make our requests known to Him, and leave them in His hands, He'll give us peace.

Father, because You hold all the answers,
help me to rest in You when life gets tough.
In Jesus's name, amen.

I beg you to recognize the extreme simplicity of faith; it is
nothing more nor less than just believing God when He says
He either has done something for us, or will do it; and then
trusting Him to do it. It is so simple that it is hard to explain.

HANNAH WHITALL SMITH

Anxiety does not empty tomorrow
of its sorrows, but only
empties today of its strength.

CHARLES SPURGEON

My Soul Needs a Rest

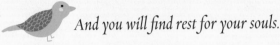

And you will find rest for your souls.

MATTHEW 11:29 NKJV

As the beach umbrella flapped gently in the wind, I soaked in the sounds around me. Seagulls squawking as they glided overhead. The crash of the waves as they broke onto the shore. My grandchildren laughing as they played in the water. The whisper of the ocean breezes as they wafted by.

Warm sunshine shone down on me, relaxing muscles that had been tight with tension when I arrived that day. You see, when our family vacation finally began, I was weary. Physically. Emotionally. And, yes, even spiritually.

Long months of illness had taken their toll. My sixteenth surgical procedure had arrived unexpectedly in the form of emergency eye surgery that left me on bed rest for several weeks. I'd used up all my reserves emotionally. It felt like there was nothing left.

But as I sat on the sand that day with my family, I felt a sweet peace seep into my soul. I rested, soaking in the beauty of His creation, looking at the majesty and grandness of the ocean, and was reminded once again of the majesty and grandness of a God who can bring rest to our souls.

Father, thank You for sending moments
that bring sweet rest to our souls. Amen.

If there be anything that can render the soul calm,
dissipate its scruples and dispel its fears,
sweeten its sufferings by the anointing of love,
impart strength to all its actions, and spread abroad
the joy of the Holy Spirit in its countenance and words,
it is this simple and childlike repose in the arms of God.

S. D. GORDON

The everlasting God, the Lord, the Creator
of the ends of the earth, neither faints nor is
weary. His understanding is unsearchable.
He gives power to the weak, and to those
who have no might He increases strength.

ISAIAH 40:28–29 NKJV

Elijah and the Thin Quiet

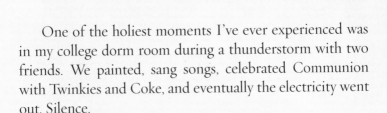

After the fire, there was a sound. Thin. Quiet.

1 KINGS 19:12 CEB

One of the holiest moments I've ever experienced was in my college dorm room during a thunderstorm with two friends. We painted, sang songs, celebrated Communion with Twinkies and Coke, and eventually the electricity went out. Silence.

Sometimes I expect to encounter God's presence in grandiose ways, but more often than not, it's simpler than that.

God told Elijah to stand at the base of a mountain for God to pass by.

A strong wind tore through the mountains. Elijah searched for God in the wind, but no luck. After the wind came an earthquake, but God wasn't there. Then came a fire, burning trees and the ground around him. God wasn't there either. But after the fire, there was calm. The Hebrew word is sometimes translated as "thin. Quiet."

God shows up unexpectedly in the simplicity of our lives—in the mundane, unspectacular, and routine. When we recognize God in the thin quiet, life becomes sacramental. Your experiences, relationships, struggles, and joys are drenched in the divine. The secular becomes sacred, the mundane becomes holy, and the boring becomes beautiful.

God of the thin quiet, pass by me today even in the seemingly mundane parts. Help me to remember that You are with me always.

I have learned by some experience, by many examples, and by the writings of countless others before me, also occupied in the search, that certain environments, certain modes of life, certain rules of conduct are more conducive to inner and outer harmony than others....
Simplification of life is one of them.

ANN MORROW LINDBERGH

He has shown you, O mortal, what is good. And what does the Lord require of you? To act justly and to love mercy and to walk humbly with your God.

MICAH 6:8 NIV

Righteousness = Peace

*The fruit of...righteousness will be peace;
its effect will be quietness and confidence forever.*

ISAIAH 32:17 NIV

Have you ever had one of those sleepless nights when you replayed the day's events, reviewing what you said, what you should have done, what you forgot to do, what you wish you could do over? Those nights usually spring from our regrets.

Doing the right thing is not always easy. Sometimes we feel pressure to cut corners, to compromise standards, to have a bad attitude, or to adopt the world's value system. But the Lord tells us that when we plant righteousness or right living, we will reap peace. When we do what is right, we sleep at night. We have peace of mind and quietness of heart.

So how can we know in advance what is the right thing? We must be saturated in God's Word, sensitive to the Spirit's direction, and committed to prayer. These disciplines must be so much a part of our practice that our words and actions flow from them. The payoff is quietness, confidence, and peace, well worth the investment!

Lord, we know that the wicked are like the troubled sea (Isaiah 57:20), but You've promised that righteousness brings peace. Please help me to practice the disciplines that lead to righteous living.

Our yesterdays present irreparable things to us; it is true that we have lost opportunities which will never return, but God can transform this destructive anxiety into a constructive thoughtfulness for the future. Let the past sleep, but let it sleep on the bosom of Christ. Leave the Irreparable Past in His hands, and step out into the Irresistible Future with Him.

OSWALD CHAMBERS

I focus on this one thing: Forgetting the past and looking forward to what lies ahead, I press on to reach the end of the race and receive the heavenly prize for which God, through Christ Jesus, is calling us.

PHILIPPIANS 3:13–14 NLT

Identifying My Chariots

Some trust in chariots and some in horses,
but we trust in the name of the Lord our God.

PSALM 20:7 NIV

I really thought I had a strong faith. Then life came crashing down around me. The crash didn't happen all at once. It started small, like a rockslide of pebbles. The irritations began to add up, and the stress increased. The challenges became larger and it wasn't long before my life felt like it was sliding toward a major crash. It got to the point where I started each day with a sense of dread that something else would go wrong.

I began to work out contingency plans. I'd try to anticipate what was coming and work out solutions. It was an exhausting way to live. During my devotion time one morning, I read this verse. It hit me that all my plans were just chariots and horses.

I was trusting in the things I could see and touch—finances, friends, and my own abilities to anticipate every scenario. I gave up my worrying and turned to God for strength when things were piling up. I still had struggles, but now I had peace as my foundation and that made all the difference.

Dear Lord, help me to always trust You first when my life gets difficult. Amen.

Approach this day with awareness of who is boss. As you make plans for the day, remember that it is I who orchestrate the events of your life. On days when things go smoothly, according to your plans, you may be unaware of My sovereign Presence. On days when your plans are thwarted, be on the lookout for Me! I may be doing something important in your life, something quite different from what you expected.

SARAH YOUNG

With him is an arm of flesh; but with us is the Lord our God, to help us and to fight our battles.

2 CHRONICLES 32:8 NKJV

The God Who Sees

Hagar used another name to refer to the LORD...
"You are the God who sees me."

GENESIS 16:13 NLT

Whether we've actually run away or not, I imagine we've all fantasized about it. Hurts, hopelessness, shame... They can make us feel that we are all alone or that we'd rather be! Hagar was no different. She ran away from her mistress, Sarai, and God asked her, *"Where have you come from, and where are you going?"* Even this question carries with it *hope*. Hagar has a future and God can see it! As she considers going back into the chaos, she's bolstered by this thought: *"The God Who Sees Me" goes with me. He knows all about me and is attuned to my needs. He's watching over me and caring for me. I am not abandoned and alone.*

As Jesus taught in Matthew 6:25–32, Hagar found some solace and peace in the thoughts that she was valuable enough for God to notice her and God was caring for her. With those truths, she went back into the chaos of life and faced whatever came. Do you know the *God Who Sees* and that He cares for you even in your chaos?

God, give me the peace You speak of and assurance of my value in Your eyes.

O Lord, You have searched me and known me.
You know my sitting down and my rising up;
You understand my thought afar off....
Where can I go from Your Spirit?
Or where can I flee from Your presence?

PSALM 139:1–2, 7 NKJV

Snuggle in God's arms. When you are hurting, when you feel lonely, left out, let Him cradle you, comfort you, reassure you of His all-sufficient power and love.

KAY ARTHUR

Overcome by Peace

Peace I leave with you; my peace I give to you.
Not as the world gives do I give to you.
Let not your hearts be troubled, neither let them be afraid.

JOHN 14:27 ESV

As I sat on the sofa with my open Bible in my lap, I was overcome by fear and despair. Searching through the pages, I was unable to find anything to speak to the situation I was facing. Blinded by tears, I called out to God, wondering where He was and why He seemed so far away. I even began to doubt my faith and desperately asked for a Scripture that would show me He was real. I closed my Bible, reopened it with closed eyes, and put my finger on the page. When I opened my eyes, my finger rested on a verse telling me to call on Him in my time of trouble.

Wow! Instantly I began to praise Him, tears streaming down my face in thankfulness, as peace descended on me, a peace such as I had never felt before. My fear was gone, and I no longer felt despair. Suddenly peace reigned; no longer did my situation envelop me in hopelessness.

Lord of peace and comfort,
thank You for the peace You give to us
when we call on You. Amen.

The entrance of Your words gives light.

PSALM 119:130 NKJV

I love the Lord, for he heard my voice;
he heard my cry for mercy. Because he turned his ear to me,
I will call on him as long as I live.

PSALM 116:1–2 NIV

Be sure of this: I am with you always,
even to the end of the age.

MATTHEW 28:20 NLT

The Promise of Perfect Peace

You will keep in perfect peace those whose minds are steadfast, because they trust in you.

ISAIAH 26:3 NIV

The little kangaroo in its mother's pouch provides a lesson in trust. Flying through the outback, the mother runs up to 40 miles per hour. In God's ingenious design, the opening of the pouch faces upward, preventing the baby from falling out even at high speeds. The cozy pocket keeps the joey secure as he goes along for the ride, providing a warm, safe place for him to grow up. Imagine the bouncing, the jolting, the jarring of a ride in a kangaroo pouch. Anchored firmly, the baby kangaroo remains tucked away, intuitively understanding steadfast trust. And when he is ready, he emerges, unscathed, ready to bounce on his own.

Human beings could learn from this tiny creature of the Australian outback. We need firm mooring, a place of security and safety amidst the bumps and jolts of life. God has designed for us a way to find that shelter. When we trust God, fixing our minds upon Him, we are promised perfect peace. Like a little joey in its mother's pouch, we are carried by One much stronger and wiser than us, and our minds are guarded with God's perfect peace.

Lord, help me choose to fix my mind on You,
trusting You steadfastly today. Amen.

Blessed is the one who trusts in the Lord, whose confidence
is in him. They will be like a tree planted by the water
that sends out its roots by the stream. It does not fear
when heat comes; its leaves are always green. It has no worries
in a year of drought and never fails to bear fruit.

JEREMIAH 17:7–8 NIV

As many have learned and later taught,
you don't realize Jesus is all you need
until Jesus is all you have.

TIM KELLER

Why, God?

"For My thoughts are not your thoughts, nor are your ways My ways," says the Lord. "For as the heavens are higher than the earth, so are My ways higher than your ways, and My thoughts than your thoughts."

ISAIAH 55:8–9 NKJV

Sometimes things happen to us that we don't understand. All of us have been through hard times and dealt with difficult or heart-breaking circumstances. Sometimes we can make sense of the situations, but on many occasions, the cry on our hearts is "Why, God? Why?"

I felt that way when I got the horrible news of my dad's suicide, after the car wreck that almost took our lives and left me in the hospital for weeks, and when faced with my adult son's chronic illness—one that has affected his life in major ways. I'm a "fixer" by nature. When something's wrong, I jump into action to fix it—but these were things that I couldn't make better.

But those were the situations that taught me to trust Him—and years later, I've realized that those were the times I felt closest to Him, when He gave me an unexplainable peace, and when I realized that He was "enough" for whatever situation I was facing.

*Father, remind me that even when
I don't understand the circumstances,
I can still trust You.*

Do not strive in your own strength; cast yourself at the feet
of the Lord Jesus, and wait upon Him in the sure confidence
that He is with you, and works in you. Strive in prayer;
let faith fill your heart so will you be strong in the Lord,
and in the power of His might.

ANDREW MURRAY

*His divine power has given us everything
we need for a godly life through
our knowledge of him who called us
by his own glory and goodness.*

2 PETER 1:3 NIV

The Right Direction

*Trust in the Lord with all your heart; do not depend
on your own understanding. Seek his will in all you do,
and he will show you which path to take.*

PROVERBS 3:5–6 NLT

My mother called it the "cloud of confusion," that moment when you desperately want to make the right, the *absolutely right* decision...but have no idea what to do next. Instead, you freeze, your mind so overwhelmed with details, facts, and possibilities that you can't hear the advice of your friends, much less the gentle nudges and whispers of God.

Mother's words during times like these were always the same: "Stop. Sit still. Listen. Trust is never easy; it's not our nature. But you have to believe that God will open the right doors and close the wrong ones." She was always right; He always did. Once I stopped worrying and started praying, God showed the way.

Finding a place of quiet when life is frantic can seem impossible. But frenzied confusion is the enemy of trust, and trusting God is the one certain way to peace...and the ability to make the right decision.

Lord, I ask You to send me a heart of peace
and a mind of trust. Following You is the true
way to make the best choices in life. Amen.

Christ's invitation to the weary and heavy-laden
is a call to begin life over again upon a new principle—
upon His own principle. "Watch My way of doing things,"
He says. "Follow Me. Take life as I take it.
Be meek and lowly, and you will find Rest."

HENRY DRUMMOND

Be still before the Lord
and wait patiently for him.

PSALM 37:7 NIV

Am I Right?

Finally, brothers and sisters, whatever is true, whatever is noble, whatever is right, whatever is pure, whatever is lovely, whatever is admirable—if anything is excellent or praiseworthy—think about such things. Whatever you have learned or received or heard from me, or seen in me— put it into practice. And the God of peace will be with you.

PHILIPPIANS 4:8–9 NIV

The small details of everyday life have a way of crowding out everything else in our minds. The hectic morning routine gives way to work, to-do lists, schedules, and deadlines. Evenings become cluttered with all the tasks that keep a household running smoothly. Even relationships give way to the drive of "what comes next"—especially our relationship with Christ.

Paul, in Philippians 4, recommended a step back, a refocusing on what's truly important. He knew that our thoughts become our behavior, and he never wanted the ways of the world to overtake our relationship with the Lord.

What joy Paul had in Christ! In Philippians 4, the words seem to bounce right off the page as he proclaimed in verse 4: "Rejoice in the Lord always. I will say it again: Rejoice!" He wanted everyone to experience this, so he passed on instructions that would bring believers joy...and, ultimately, peace.

*Lord, whenever the world swamps us
with details, help us keep our focus on You.
Guide us with Your wisdom and pass
on to us Your peace. Amen.*

You can have as much of Me and My peace
as you want, through thousands of correct choices
each day. The most persistent choice you face
is whether to trust Me or to worry. You will never
run out of things to worry about, but you can choose
to trust Me no matter what. I am an ever-present help
in trouble. Trust Me, though the earth give way
and the mountains fall into the heart of the sea.

SARAH YOUNG